THE TENTS OF BALTIMORE

Ohelim in the Jewish Cemeteries

I0027157

Dianne Weiner Feldman and Nancy Stark Schoenburg

HERITAGE BOOKS
2011

HERITAGE BOOKS

AN IMPRINT OF HERITAGE BOOKS, INC.

Books, CDs, and more—Worldwide

For our listing of thousands of titles see our website
at
www.HeritageBooks.com

Published 2011 by
HERITAGE BOOKS, INC.
Publishing Division
100 Railroad Ave. #104
Westminster, Maryland 21157

Copyright © 2011 Dianne Weiner Feldman
and Nancy Stark Schoenburg

*Photographs by Dianne Weiner Feldman
in 2010 unless otherwise indicated.*

All rights reserved. No part of this book may be reproduced or
transmitted in any form or by any means, electronic or mechanical,
including photocopying, recording or by any information storage
and retrieval system without written permission from the authors,
except for the inclusion of brief quotations in a review.

International Standard Book Numbers
Paperbound: 978-0-7884-5291-8
Clothbound: 978-0-7884-8687-6

The historic built environment is frequently the only tangible evidence of history, and historic structures can open new doors to understanding the past. They can be significant for their characteristics and features as well as for their association with people and events.

John A. Burns, editor of *Recording Historic Structures*, 2007

But monuments themselves memorials need.

George Crabbe: *The Borough (Letter 2)*, 1810

Contents

Preface

Tucked away in several cemeteries of Baltimore are
memorial structures that quietly hold a piece of Jewish history. The small buildings cover graves of various rabbis and rebbitzens, as well as some non-
clergy. Such a structure is called an *ohel* (plural,
ohelim), meaning tent in Hebrew. An ohel is an en-
closed structure built over an in–ground burial. The
ohel is different from a mausoleum, a structure in
which there is an above–ground interment.

Family members, congregants, students and friends
might visit the ohelim on a yahrzeit and before Rosh
HaShanah and sometimes at other times of the year.
Visiting gravesites of prominent rabbis to pray and
meditate is a tradition of some Jewish communities.
In Israel, religious and secular Jews alike go to pray
at the ohelim, tombs and graves of the sages.
Groups travel overseas to the graves of their rebbes
and to some ohelim in the United States, especially
in the New York City area. In a few cases, groups
have come to Baltimore from other cities to visit an
ohel.

The majority of individuals whose ohelim are dis-
played in this booklet were born in Eastern Europe
and passed away between the 1930s and 1950s, although the earliest died in 1892 and the most recent
in 1963. Over the years some of the ohelim have
been maintained, while others have deteriorated.
Some have significant cracks in the structure and
holes in the roof. All that is left of one is the con-

crete frame on the ground around the site. In a few years others may no longer be standing.

This material culture of Baltimore Jewry should not just disappear unnoticed. Therefore, we are pleased to present herein photos and descriptions of ohelim from some of the Jewish cemeteries in Baltimore, Maryland. May this help to preserve the memory of a part of Baltimore history, the ohelim and the names of those they honor.

Dianne Weiner Feldman
Nancy Stark Schoenburg

ROSEDALE CEMETERY

Rabbi Hillel and Rebbitzen Ida Mihaly

Location: Tifereth Israel Anshe Sphard section of the Rosedale Cemetery, 6300 Hamilton Avenue, Rosedale, MD. Entrance is on Hamilton Avenue, opposite Montrose and Roseland Avenues.

Description: The building is pale brick outside and red brick inside with a corrugated metal ceiling, flat roof, a window on each side and metal gate with Star of David on top. The metal bars across the windows match the gate. The plaque above the doorway is engraved in Hebrew and English with the names Hillel (HaRav Hillel) Mihaly and Ida (Yehudit Miriam) Mihaly. There is a large vertical crack in the outside rear wall. Inside artificial grass carpeting surrounds the graves. There are two interior inset memorial plaques which are stained.

Dimensions: 7' x 7'–9" x 7'–7"

Condition: Good

Notes from the plaques:
Rabbi Mihaly: The upper section of the plaque is a poem in the form of an acrostic with the first letter of each line in sequence spelling Hillel ben Aryeh. It praises Rabbi Mihaly as being a pious, humble and righteous person.

Rabbi Mihaly

4

His children are left without his guidance as their teacher. He was a master of Torah, very devout, and charitable. Lower section: Rabbi Hillel son of Rabbi Aryeh Mihaly (Michaeli) taught righteousness in his congregation,
Tifereth Israel, for 33 years of his life. He died with a
good name on the second day of Chol Hamoed Pesach, 18
Nissan 5717, April 19, 1957. May his soul be bound up in
the bond of everlasting life.

Rebbitzen Mihaly: Our dear mother, a woman of valor,
the crown of her husband and the glory of her children; a

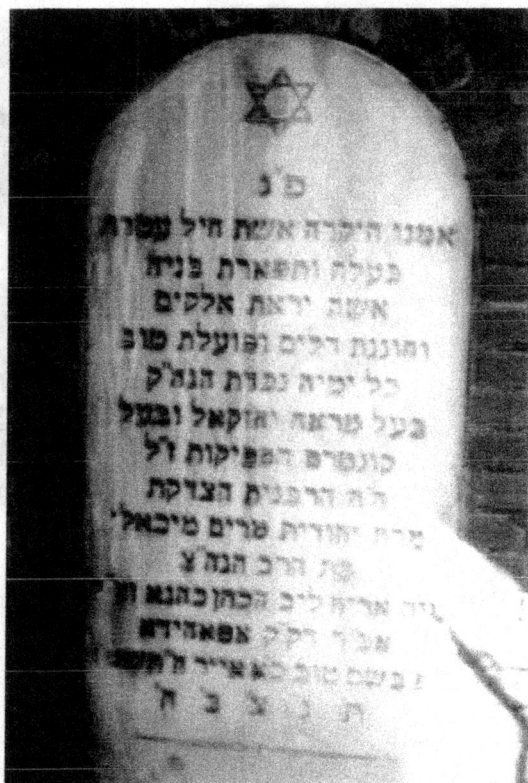

Rebbitzen Mihaly

God–fearing woman, kind to the poor, a worker for good all the days of her life. She was the granddaughter of the learned rabbi who wrote *Ma'reh Yechezkel* and *Kuntras HaSfikot*. [Author of these texts was Rabbi Yehuda Yosef Kahan.] May their memory be a blessing. Mrs. Yehudit Miriam Mihaly (Ida) was the daughter of Rabbi Aryeh Leib HaCohen Kahan, of blessed memory, of the religious court of the holy community of Apahida. She died with a good name on 21 Iyar 5715, May 13, 1955. May her soul be bound up in the bond of everlasting life.

Historical notes: According to the current caretaker, Mr. Paul Karp, this was the last ohel built in the Rosedale Cemetery.

Synagogues, Temples and Congregations of Maryland by Earl Pruce reports that Rabbi Mihaly was installed as the spiritual leader of Tifereth Israel Anshe Sphard on June 9, 1929.

The April 22, 1957, *Sun* paper summarized Rabbi Mihaly's accomplishments: he had led Tifereth Israel Anshe Sphard for more than 30 years; he was chairman of the Orthodox rabbinical organization in Baltimore; he was one of the founders of Vaad Hakashruth; he served as chairman of the Hebrew Talmudical Academy and was one of the founders of the Bais Yaakov School for Girls.

Rabbi Abraham Nachman Schwartz

Location: Shomrei Mishmeres section of Rosedale Cemetery, 6300 Hamilton Avenue, Rosedale, MD. Shomrei Mishmeres has three sections at Rosedale. This section of Shomrei Mishmeres is on the west side of Hamilton Avenue near the old cemetery office and chapel. The ohel is very near Rabbi Israel Zvi Karen's ohel.

Description: The building is constructed of light–colored brick with a darker red brick Star of David above the doorway. There is a metal gate with a Star of David design near the top and two narrow barred windows on either side of the gate. Two white memorial tablets are mounted outside below the windows. The roof has a slight pitch. The interior of the ohel has weeds, a tree and trash. The outline of the grave is not visible.

Dimensions: 5' x 9'–2" x 8' (parapet not included)

Condition: Good

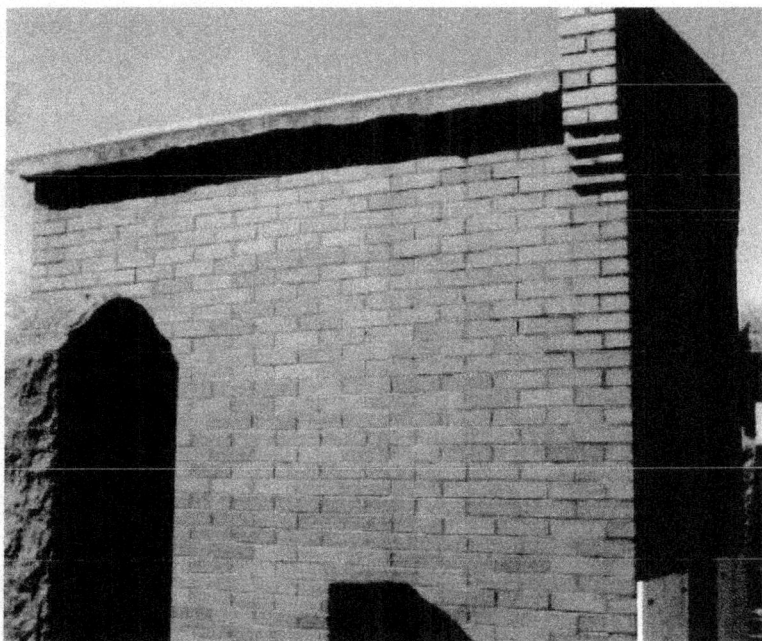

Notes from the plaques: Our master, our teacher, and our rav, Rabbi Avraham Nachman son of Chaim Schwartz, may his memory be a blessing; head of the Beit Din (religious court) of Baltimore. The crown has been taken from our head. Rabbi Schwartz passed away on 23 Shevat 5697, Thursday, February 4, 1937. May his soul be bound up in the bond of everlasting life.

Historical Notes: Founder of the Hebrew Parochial School, forerunner of the Talmudical Academy of Baltimore.

The February 5, 1937, *Sun* paper contained an obituary for Rabbi Schwartz which states he was the founder and dean of the Hebrew Parochial School, 1709 East Baltimore Street. As the funeral procession passed the school en route to the cemetery, the school children were going to offer a prayer. Due to the large crowd anticipated, Rabbi Schwartz's funeral was to be held on the outside of Shomrei Mishmeres Synagogue and rabbis of New York City were going to attend.

Synagogues, Temples and Congregations of Maryland by Earl Pruce recounts the naming of a synagogue in memory of Rabbi Schwartz. The synagogue, Zichron Abraham Nachman Anshe Sphard, went out of existence in the late 1950s.

Rabbi Israel Zvi Karen

Location: Shomrei Mishmeres section of the Rosedale Cemetery, 6300 Hamilton Avenue, Rosedale, MD. There are three sections of Shomrei Mishmeres in Rosedale. This section is on the west side of Hamilton Avenue between the old cemetery office/chapel and the former caretaker's home, near the ohel of Rabbi Abraham Nachman Schwartz.

11

Description: The ohel is built of block covered with a veneer. There is a solid metal door and cement roof. Red brick surmounted on the roof over the door holds a white stone memorial tablet with two Stars of David. No grave outline is visible in the uneven dirt floor.

Dimensions: 4' x 8' x 5'

Condition: Poor. Several cinder blocks have chunks missing and the door does not close securely.

left side, back of parapet and plaque

Notes from the plaque (over front door of ohel): Here lies a righteous and honest man who did charitable works until his death. The learned rav, our honored master and scholar, Rabbi Yisrael Zvi son of Toby (HaLevy) Karen, died while still in his prime on 8 Sivan 5692, June

12

12, 1932. May his soul be bound up in the bond of everlasting life.

Historical Notes: The June 13, 1932, *Sun* reported that Israel Karem *[sic]* was struck by an automobile on Saturday afternoon and died on Sunday. Rabbi Karem had been in this country seven weeks. He arrived in Baltimore on Friday after being in New York. According to the *Sun*, the rabbi spent Saturday morning giving talks in various synagogues on behalf of the Rabbinical Institution of Lithuania. He was struck after leaving one of the synagogues. Rabbi Karem was born in Russia, where his widow and two children were still living.

The *Sun* states further that Rabbi Karem was buried in the Shomrei Mishmeres Congregation cemetery with Rabbi Abraham N. Schwartz officiating. The rabbi's brothers, Selig and Morris, of New York and his brother–in–law Rabbi B. Aronowitz of Yeshiva College in New York were expected to attend the funeral.

Newspaper references to the accident spelled his name "Karem." However, his death certificate, funeral home record and the plaque at the ohel used the spelling "Karen."

Rabbi Morris Marcus

Location: Ohr Knesseth Israel section of Rosedale Cemetery, 6300 Hamilton Avenue, Rosedale, MD. This ohel is very near the old chapel/cemetery office.

Description: This is a block building with slightly rounded cement roof, small rusted metal door, white memorial tablet inset on outside rear wall and no windows. The top hinge on the door is broken. It appears extra cement has been applied to the doorjamb and red bricks

14

cemented to the bottom of the doorway to prevent the door from opening.

Dimensions: 4' x 8' x 5'

Condition: Appears solid but there are cracks in the blocks and the door has some holes in it.

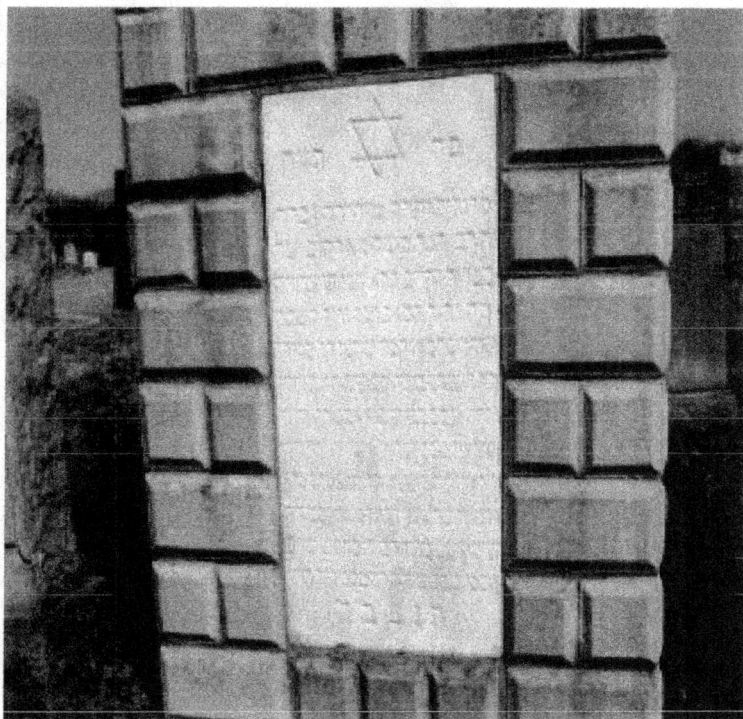

Notes from the plaque: Here lies a precious jewel, shining and pure; the learned Rabbi Moshe Marcus of blessed memory. May his soul be bound up in eternal life. How great is the pain and how great is the calamity. The great scholar, a man of only 42 years, his tender children left without a father, teacher, guide. Rabbi Marcus guided Ohr Knesseth Israel Congregation for about five years with Torah scholarship and piety. Tears are shed like a river. Rabbi Marcus passed away at age 42 on 5 Tevet 5690, January 5, 1930. May his soul be bound up in the bond of everlasting life.

Historical Notes: The January 6, 1930, *Sun* paper reported that Rabbi Marcus died at Sinai Hospital after a two week stay. Additional biographical information from the obituary states that "he came to Baltimore from Lithuania, where he studied at the Telse and Slobodka Yeshivas. He was among the leading Talmudical scholars of the day." He taught at the Baltimore Hebrew Talmudical Seminary on East Baltimore Street.

According to the newspaper account, "Rabbi Marcus died on the wedding day of his namesake Morris Marcus, son of his brother, Rabbi Joseph Marcus of the Mishkon Israel Synagogue." Services were held in the deceased's home, followed by services in Ohr Knesseth Israel Synagogue. The Ohr Knesseth Israel Synagogue services were followed by services in Mishkon Israel Synagogue.

There is an ohel honoring Rabbi Joseph Marcus, who is thought to have been Rabbi Morris Marcus' brother, in the Mishkon Israel section of the cemetery on Southern Ave. However, the name of Rabbi Morris Marcus' father does not appear on the plaque at his ohel. The plaque at the ohel of Rabbi Joseph Marcus (Yosef Yakov) does include the name of his father, Rabbi Ziskind Marcus.

Isreal *[sic]* and Fannie Rivkin

Location: Rosedale Cemetery, 6300 Hamilton Avenue, Rosedale, MD. This building is very near the old chapel/cemetery office.

Description: The structure appears to have been built in stages. Two different types of brick were used, and there are separate roofs. There is no door. Windows on both sides are divided by bricks.

Dimensions: 8' x 6'–6" x 5'

Condition: Good

Notes from the plaques: Isreal Rivkin: To the memory of our father: Isreal son of Issachar Rivkin, died on 9 Tevet 5680, December 31, 1919. May his soul be bound up in the bond of everlasting life.

Fannie Rivkin: To the memory of our mother: Esther Feigle Rivkin daughter of Eli, died 24 Nissan 5688, April 14, 1928. May her soul be bound up in the bond of everlasting life.

Historical Notes: The 1900 U.S. census record shows that "Issie Rivkin" was born in 1854 in Russia and Fannie in 1863 (also in Russia). He came to the United States in 1890 and Fannie in 1894.

Rabbi I. B. and Rebbitzen Chava Isaacson

Location: Beth Hamedrosh Hagodol section of the Rosedale Cemetery, 6300 Hamilton Avenue, Rosedale, MD. Enter through the archway on the Philadelphia Road side of the cemetery.

Description: This building has a white brick exterior and red brick interior with a wrought iron gate covering the doorway. There is an inset plaque over the door with the inscription "Rabbi I. B. Isaacson and Wife" flanked on both sides by a Star of David. There are two barred windows on either side of the doorway, two larger windows on either side of structure and two inset memorial tablets on the exterior rear wall. The roof is made of a green corrugated material. A cement floor surrounds the graves inside. The grave on the left bears the name "Mother." The one on the right says "Father." Some brick repair has been done near the top of the building. The ceiling has been whitewashed. The white outer finish is peeling in a number of places. The ohel is surrounded by other burials with the surname Isaacson.

Dimensions: 9'–10" x 9'–2" x 8'

Condition: Good

Notes from the plaques: Tombstone of our dear father, learned teacher and master, Rabbi Yitzhak Ben–Zion son of Shimon Isaacson. May his memory be a blessing. An honest man, dweller of the tent of Torah. He served in the Baltimore rabbinate for 25 years. Rabbi Isaacson died at the age of 70 on 21 Av 5691, August 4, 1931. May his soul be bound up in the bond of everlasting life.

Tombstone of our dear and modest mother, Rebbitzen Chava Dusha Isaacson, daughter of Yehuda. May her memory be a blessing. A woman of valor and God–fearing, she died at the age of 67 on Erev Shabbat, 17 Adar II 5692, March 25, 1932. May her soul be bound up in the bond of everlasting life.

Historical Notes: From *A Pictorial History of Maryland Jewry* compiled and edited by A. D. Glushakow, "Rabbi Isaacson was the first rabbi of Beth Hamedrosh Hagodol Congregation. He began immediately upon his arrival in Baltimore in 1905 and served the congregation for more than a quarter of a century until his death in 1931. For a number of years, he was the Dean of the Baltimore Rabbinate."

Rabbi Samuel Liebb

Location: Beth Hamedrosh Hagodol section of the Rosedale Cemetery, 6300 Hamilton Avenue, Rosedale, MD. Enter through the arch on Philadelphia Road side of the cemetery. This ohel is on the left side of the driveway.

Description: The structure is made of white glossy bricks that are similar to those used for Rabbi Isaacson's ohel. There is a red roof, windows with iron bars on each side of the building, a doorway with a metal gate and an exterior rear memorial tablet. Cement surrounds the grave inside; however, a tree is growing in the crack between the cement and the side of the grave.

Dimensions: 6'–8" x 7'–10" x 7'–10"

Condition: Good. The original roof and parapets have been replaced.

Notes from the plaque: Our dear father, Rabbi Shmuel Yitzhak Liebb, may his memory be a blessing. He dwelt in the tent of Torah. He served as rabbi of Beth Hamedrosh Hagodol in Baltimore. He died on 25 Kislev 5701, December 25, 1940. Rabbi Shmuel Yitzhak was the son of Zevulon. May his soul be bound up in the bond of everlasting life.

Historical notes: From *Synagogues, Temples and Congregations of Maryland* by Earl Pruce, "Rabbi Liebb was the rabbi at the time of Beth Hamedrosh Hagodol Agudas Achim's dedication of a new building, 204 East Baltimore Street on March 21, 1937."

Israel Benesch and Jacob Benesch

Location: Beth Hamedrosh Hagodol section of the Rosedale Cemetery, 6300 Hamilton Street, Rosedale, MD. Enter through the arch on the Philadelphia Road side of the cemetery. The ohel is on the right near the top of the rise in the land.

Description: The brick of this building is light brown. The name above the door is spelled BENESCH; however, the two memorial tablets on either side of the doorway spell the name as BENESH. There is a metal gate which appears new in the doorway and barred windows on the sides. The doorstep says BENESCH. As you look through the gate, the grave and upright memorial stone for Jacob are on the right. The information on the stone is duplicated on the outside memorial plaque. Israel's grave on the left bears a plaque stating "at rest."

Dimension: 7' x 8' x 9'

Condition: Good; an outside crack and the ceiling have been repaired.

Notes from the plaques: Jacob Benesh: Our beloved father and teacher, Yakov Yehuda son of Zvi Yitzhak, died on 23 Elul 5678, September 1, 1918, at age 85.

Although the plaque states the date of death as September 1, 1918, in English, the Maryland State Archives Death Index has his date of death as August 31, 1918. Moreover, the Hebrew date of 23 Elul 5678 corresponds to August 31, 1918 (or August 30, 1918, if he had passed away after sundown).

Israel Benesh: Our beloved father and teacher, Yisrael Yuda son of Yakov Yehuda, died on 6 Shevat 5702, January 24, 1942, at age 76.

Over the front door: Lovely and pleasant in their life, even in their death they were not separated.

Historical Notes: The January 25, 1942, *Sun* newspaper death notice for Israel Benesch of 651 West Lexington Street stated he was the husband of Ida and the father of nine children. The Jewish Museum of Maryland has in its collection a photograph of Israel Benesch, a Russian immigrant who owned a haberdashery at 651 W. Lexington Street. The museum also has a photograph of Ida Benesch.

Yehuda and Sarah Barrash

Location: Mogen Abraham section of the Rosedale Cemetery, 6300 Hamilton Avenue, Rosedale, MD. Enter through the arch on the Philadelphia Road side of the cemetery.

Description: Large stone blocks with two pillars at the entrance. The name Barrash is above the columns and a Star of David is above the name. Two steps lead up to the wrought iron door which has been screened. The outside back wall has two inset plaques. There are windows covered with bars on either side of the structure. A small backless stone bench with the name Barrash is in front. One support of the bench appears to have shifted.

There are two graves inside. The grave on the left has a sign indicating "Father" and the grave on the right has a sign engraved "Mother."

Dimensions: 9'–9" x 12'–9" x 9'–8"

Condition: Good

Notes from the plaques: *For his plaque, the first letter of each line taken in sequence forms the acrostic Yehuda Moshe, and for hers it spells out Sarah Leah.*

Yehuda Moshe son of Uriah: His wife, children and grandchildren mourn his death. The crown has been taken from their heads, and they remain alone; his memory will not perish ever from their hearts; his ways and his actions are exemplary to all. The echo remains in their hearts. He hastened to help the poor and the beggar with money and aid. The memorial was raised after his death. His name was sanctified by the naming *[in his honor]* of Congregation Beth Yehuda, which was built with his funds. He passed away on 9 Shevat 5694, January 25, 1934. May his soul be bound up in the bond of everlasting life. 1871 – 1934

Sarah Leah daughter of Nachman Manis: Our mother Sarah, the crown of our head and of our families, raised a large family to honor and splendor and was as compassionate as a mother to her grandchildren and relations. We will never forget you — remembering you before our eyes, loving peace, charity, and righteousness as you taught us. They are engraved on our hearts always. She died on 17 Elul 5710, August 30, 1950. May her soul be bound up in the bond of everlasting life. 1874 – 1950

Historical notes: *A Pictorial History of Maryland Jewry* compiled and edited by A. D. Glushakow relates that, "During the spring of 1934, Frank Barrash representing the Yehuda M. Barrash family, made a generous contribution to the Forest Park Hebrew Congregation. In recognition, the synagogue changed its name to Beth Yehuda in memory of the father of the Barrash family."

BOWLEY'S LANE CEMETERY

HERRING RUN

Rabbi Solomon and Rebbitzen Gittel Kruger

Location: Ohel Yakov section of the cemeteries located at 6700 Bowley's Lane (aka Herring Run Cemetery), Baltimore, MD. Enter the cemetery through the Ohel Yakov arch. The ohel is at the end of the lane.

Description: This red brick structure sits between two sidewalks. There are two peeling plaques with Hebrew writing on the outside of the building, two wrought iron gates on the far side, two 3' x 2' barred windows on either side, six half columns on the outside of the building, pitched roof with slate shingles, and a metal plaque mounted with the names Solomon Kruger and Gittel Kruger on an inside wall. Two bricks on the plaque side of the structure show a brickmaker's mark, LS.Ton N, stamped on them.

Dimensions: 15' x 10'–3" x 8'–8"

Condition: Good

Notes from the plaques: Tombstone of our father, teacher of righteousness, laws of God and His Torah; from a line of learned scholars, masters of Torah. Our honored master, scholar and rav, the distinguished Rabbi Yekutiel Zalman, son of the learned Rabbi Yosef Mordechai Krieger (Kruger), who served in the Baltimore rabbinate for 16 years. He passed away on Shabbat Kodesh, 15 Cheshvan 5680, November 8, 1919, and was buried on Sunday the ninth. May his soul be bound up in the bond of everlasting life.

The tombstone of our mother, a modest and beloved woman, crowned in every measure of righteousness, a woman of valor, God–fearing and pure, Rebbitzen Gittel Krieger, i.e. Kruger, daughter of Yakov, died on 5 Tevet 5697, December 19, 1936. May her soul be bound up in the bond of everlasting life.

[Inside the ohel is a wall plaque in English and Hebrew: Dedicated to the sacred memory of Rabbi Solomon Kruger November 8, 1919, Gittle *[sic]* Kruger December 19, 1936.]

Historical Notes: The *New York Times* of November 9, 1919, printed an obituary which read in part, "Rabbi Kruger was born in Russia in 1864 and emigrated to the U.S. in 1904...Since he took charge of the Oell *[sic]* Jacob Synagogue he had been one of the best–known orthodox rabbis in the city and wielded a large influence among the Jewish people of East Baltimore."

Rabbi Moshe and Rebbitzen Esther Rabinowitz

Location: Ohel Yakov Congregation section of the cemetery located at 6700 Bowley's Lane, aka Herring Run Cemetery. Enter the cemetery through the Ohel Yakov arch.

Description: Beige or sand colored brick. The metal gate at the doorway is flanked by two plaques that appear newer than the building, as the plaques are not stained or marked. There are blind windows on both sides and a flat roof. Evergreen trees are planted at each corner of the structure. Cement on the inside floor surrounds graves which are covered with flat tops about six inches off the ground. The grave cover on the left is not centered. The grave on the right for the rabbi has a weathered head-

36

stone. This headstone says HaRav Moshe Leib bar Shimon Rabinowitz. (While the headstone inside the ohel says Moshe Leib Rabinowitz, the outside plaque says Moshe Yehuda Rabinovitz.)

Dimensions: 8' x 8'–4" x 7'– 6"

Condition: Poor. Missing many bricks. The outside plaques appear newer than the rest of building.

Notes from the plaques: Tomb of the learned, honored master and scholar Rabbi Moshe Yehuda son of Rabbi Shimon Rabinowitz, may his memory be a blessing. An upright man, dwelling in the tents of Torah. Rabbi Rabinowitz served as rabbi of Ohel Yakov Synagogue in Baltimore for 18 years. He passed away on 25 Adar I in the year 5700, March 5, 1940, at the age of 60. May his soul be bound up in the bond of everlasting life.

Tomb of Rebbitzen Esther Henya daughter of Avraham. May she rest in peace. A woman of valor, God–fearing, the crown of her husband; righteousness and charity have filled all of her days. She stretched out her hands to the poor and the needy. She died at an old age on 2 Iyar 5717 at age 80, May 3, 1957. May her soul be bound up in the bond of everlasting life.

Historical Notes: *The Sun* newspaper of March 6, 1940, stated that, "Rabbi Rabinowitz came to this country 30 years ago."

B'NAI ISRAEL CEMETERY
MISHKON ISRAEL

SOUTHERN AVENUE

Rabbi Abraham Levinson

Location: B'nai Israel Cemetery, section B, 3701 Southern Avenue, Baltimore, MD.

Description: The glossy white tile or brick building has a corrugated red roof, small windows on both sides and an unlocked wrought iron gate at the doorway. The outline of the grave is not visible inside. A plaque written in Hebrew is mounted on the rear outside wall.

Dimensions: 6'–3" x 8'–3" x 6'–9"

Condition: The structure is in very poor condition with a tree or trees growing through the roof, peeling tiles and cracks in the walls.

Notes from the plaque: The tombstone of our father, the learned rav, our teacher and master, Rabbi Abba Chaim son of Yitzhak Izik, who served in the rabbinate of Baltimore for 22 years. He died on the Holy Sabbath, 23 Sivan 5672, June 8, 1912, and was buried on the ninth. May his soul be bound up in the bond of everlasting life.

Historical Notes: Rabbi Avraham [Abba Chaim] Levinson served as the rabbi of B'nai Israel Congregation for

22 years, from 1890 to 1912. Rebbitzen Levinson is buried next to the ohel.

The Sun newspaper printed an obituary for Rabbi Levinson which states in part, "he was born in Kowno, Russia, came to this country 31 years ago and settled in Rochester, New York, as a rabbi for the Leopold Street Congregation for 10 years."

Joseph Fisher

2003 photo courtesy Myrna Teck (back view)

Location: B'nai Israel Cemetery, 3701 Southern Avenue section B, Baltimore, MD.

Description: Ohel is no longer standing. All that remains are stone slabs that mark the outline of the

44

ohel's base. The broken plaque is on the ground and is difficult to read.

Notes from the plaque: *[The first letter of each line in sequence forms an acrostic spelling Yisroel.]* Mourning our father, the tears flow like water...to the poor and destitute, to all he gave sanctuary; a scholar, our father, Yisroel son of Elisha, who passed away on the second day of Rosh Hodesh Tammuz 5674, June 25, 1914.

Historical notes: Although the plaque uses only his Hebrew name Yisroel, federal census records and B'nai Israel cemetery office records use the name Joseph. He used the name Joseph Fisher in his business and daily life.

2010 plaque on ground after ohel is removed

The June 28, 1914, *Sun* paper noted that "Joseph Fisher was born in Russia 48 years ago and came to Baltimore when he was 27 years old. He became well known in the wholesale dry goods business and was a member of the Hebrew Federated Charities."

2009

Although the Joseph Fisher ohel is no longer standing, the above picture shows it when it was still located next to that of Samuel and Annie Fisher. Note the similarity between the two structures. The Joseph Fisher ohel deteriorated to the point that it had to be torn down in 2009.

Samuel Fisher and Annie Fisher

Location: B'nai Israel Cemetery, 3701 Southern Avenue, Baltimore, MD.

Description: White glossy tiles or bricks, small window on each side, arched doorway with wrought iron gate on the front left side. The right side of the front has an inset plaque (for Samuel) of polished dark stone. On the outside back wall are two tall inset plaques (one for Samuel and another for his mother, Annie Fisher) with tombstone information. The roof is green shingle.

Dimensions: 8'–8"x 8' x 9'

Condition: Fair. A small tree is growing inside the structure, the roof is missing shingles and the tiles are peeling.

Notes from the plaques: Samuel Fisher: here lies our beloved father, Shmuel son of Yisroel. He died on 14 Tishrei 5689, September 28, 1928, at age 38. May his soul be bound up in the bond of everlasting life.

On the dark plaque by the entrance to the ohel, the last two letters (aleph and lamed) in the names Shmuel and Yisroel are written as one combined letter. When written side by side or combined as one letter, the aleph and lamed form a spelling of God's name.

Annie Fisher: here lies our beloved and modest mother, Chaya Esther daughter of David. She died on the first

day of Rosh Hashanna 5690. The date in English is given as October 4, 1929, at age 64. May her soul be bound up in the bond of everlasting life.

Historical Notes: According to a plat of the cemetery, Samuel and his mother, Annie Fisher, are buried in part of a larger lot under the name of Louis Fisher. Joseph and Annie Fisher were the parents of nine children. The 1900 census for Baltimore records Joseph and Annie Fisher whose children include Louis and Samuel. The 1927 Baltimore City directory lists the Joseph Fisher Specialty Co., wholesale army and navy goods at 104 Hopkins Place. The 1928 *Sun* paper reports the business had moved from Hopkins Place to Fremont Avenue and Baltimore Street. Both Louis and Samuel were associated with the firm.

Harry and Ida Lipsitz

Location: Mishkon Israel section of the B'nai Israel cemetery, 3701 Southern Avenue, Baltimore, MD. As you enter through the arch into the cemetery, this structure is visible in the far left corner on a slight rise in the land.

Description: The ohel was once a striking white and blue structure, honoring the memory of Harry and Ida Lipsitz. The threshold stone reads in English: Harry Lipsitz. On each of the two side walls the form of a recessed window is filled with blue tiles matching those along the top and bottom of the ohel. The bright blue bricks define the door, roof and ornamental chimneys on the four corners as well as the windows. At the front doorway is a metal gate. A solid sheet of metal has been placed inside against the bottom of the gate.

Inside the ohel are the burial plots of Harry and Ida Lipsitz, as well as that of Jerome M. Shane, son of E & M Shane, born July 18, 1920, and died March 3, 1923. The stone marker has shifted and lies askew. The top of Ida's grave has also shifted some.

Dimensions: 10'– 4" x 10'– 4" x 8'–10"

Condition: Very poor. The coating on the tiles has deteriorated and is peeling off. The structure has numerous vertical and horizontal cracks.

Plaque on back of building

Notes from the plaques: Here lies Zvi Eliezer son of Yehuda Leib; Harry, died November 7, 1944 [corresponds to 21 Cheshvan 5705], age 85, father.

Here lies Sheina Chaya daughter of Shmuel HaCohen; Ida died December 9, 1937 [corresponds to 5 Tevet 5698], age 79, mother.

For the child, Jerome M. Shane, son of E. & M. Shane: The boy Yacov Meir bar Yitzhak Shane was born on July 18, 1920, and died March 3, 1923 [corresponds to 15 Adar I 5683].

Rear and side of building

Historical Notes: The 1910 U.S. census records show Harry Lipsitz was born ca. 1859 in Russia, and his wife Ida was born ca. 1858. The Lipsitz family came to the United States in 1904. Their children included Barney, Morris, Etta, Rose, Minnie, Mary and Benjamin.

Rabbi Joseph Jacob and Rebbitzen Alta Sarah Rivkah Marcus

Location: Mishkon Israel section of the B'nai Israel Cemetery, 3701 Southern Avenue, Baltimore, MD. After you enter through the arches, this structure is visible in the far left of the cemetery on a slight rise in the land.

Description: This building is yellow brick with a red brick extension at the base, red brick columns or half columns at the four corners and a double metal gate in front. Red brick steps at the outside rear lead to two inset plaques. Blind windows on either side are trimmed in red brick at the base. Green outdoor carpeting covers the graves inside.

The marble sign above the gate says, "Erected by Mr. and Mrs. Simon Needle in loving memory of Rabbi Joseph Jacob Marcus, died July 28, 1932."

Dimensions: Yellow brick portion 10'–5" x 9'–6" x 8'–1" Red brick portion at base measures 12'–10" x 10'–10"

Condition: Good

The bronze plaques shown below are not original to the ohel. They were likely added to the front columns within the past decade. These newer plaques have essentially the same inscriptions as those on the outside back wall.

Notes from the plaques: The lamp of God is the spirit of man. To the soul of our beloved father, righteous, pious and humble, a luminary of Israel, master of Torah, treasure of reverence; Admor Rabbi Yosef Yaakov son of Rabbi Ziskind Marcus, may his memory be a blessing. He passed away at age 59 on Thursday, 24 Tammuz 5692, July 28, 1932. May his soul be bound up in the bond of everlasting life.

To the memory of our dear mother, a God–fearing woman; she is to be praised. The modest Rebbitzen Alta Sarah Rivkah Marcus, daughter of Shimon, may the memory of the righteous be a blessing. She died at age 75 on Monday, 24 Iyar 5715, May 16, 1955. May her soul be bound up in the bond of everlasting life.

Historical Notes: Rabbi Marcus is believed to be a brother of Rabbi Moshe Marcus who died in 1930 and whose ohel is in the Ohr Knesseth Israel section of the Rosedale Cemetery.

The July 14, 1933, *Jewish Times* had a photo of the structure with an article, "Unveiling and Dedication of Mausoleum in Memory of Rabbi Joseph J. Marcus." The article states that Rabbi Marcus died in New Jersey while visiting relatives. He was laying tefillin at the time of his death. According to the article, Rabbi Marcus was born in Lithuania in 1874, educated at the yeshivas of Slobodka and Volojohin and ordained as a rabbi at the age of 18. After occupying various rabbinical positions in Europe, he came to Baltimore in 1922.

The *Jewish Times* article concluded by issuing an invitation to the Jews of Baltimore to participate in memorial services at the synagogue on July 15 for Rabbi Marcus and to attend the services at the cemetery on July 16.   Various rabbis and cantors of Baltimore were expected to participate in the services as well as two rabbis who were alumni of the Slobodka Yeshiva.

The photo of the ohel that accompanied the *Jewish Times* article showed a building with slightly different columns than currently exist on the structure.

Shed or Ohel?

The above unidentified brick structure has a prominent location in the Mishkon Israel section of the B'nai Israel Cemetery. It is near two ohelim; however, it is built at a right angle to them. Although tools were once stored inside, it is unusually well–built and attractive for a storage shed. No record has been found denoting the origin of the structure. There is no identifying plaque and the door faces a different direction from other ohelim in the cemetery. The entire floor seems to be covered with cement although grass and weeds are growing in some areas.

GERMAN HILL ROAD
CEMETERY

Rabbi A. E. and Rebbitzen Bracha Axelrod

Location: Tzemach Zedek section of the cemetery is located near 6800 German Hill Road, Baltimore, MD. Another name for this cemetery is Hebrew Mt. Carmel. Three large portions comprise this cemetery. Two of the portions sit across from each other on the one–way stretch of German Hill Road. The third, non–contiguous portion is separated by Boston Street and located on the portion of German Hill Road which allows two–way traffic. This ohel sits directly behind the Tzemach Zedek gatehouse on the one–way section of German Hill Road.

Description: Brick construction with barred windows on each side. There are no windows in back. On the front is a doorway with a metal gate, topped by a Star of David. An arched design frames the doorway and windows. Inside the ohel, old stained tombstone slabs are part of the wall as inset tablets. Rabbi Axelrod's stone is on the left side and on the right side is that of Rebbitzen Axelrod. A ledge inside on the left holds candles and prayer books.

Dimensions: 6'–11" x 7' x 7'–5"

Condition: Ohel appears to be in good condition; small crack on right side and on left above the windows; lateral crack on left side.

Notes from the plaques: *Over the door the tablet says*: Rabbi Avraham Eli and Rebbitzen Bracha Niesha Axelrod, may they rest in peace.

The learned, honest, chasid, Rabbi Avraham Eli son of Aharon Shlomo, who was engaged his entire life in Torah, in worship and in acts of charity; may his memory be a blessing. He served as rabbi at Tsemach Tzedek Synagogue of the Lubavitcher Chasidim in Baltimore for 28 years. Rabbi Axelrod died on Shabbat Kodesh of Parashat Terumah, 4 Adar 5712, March 1, 1952. May his soul be bound up in the bond of everlasting life.

The Rebbitzen, modest, charitable, and prominent, a God–fearing woman, she is to be praised. Mrs. Bracha Niesha daughter of Reb Yitzhak Isaac; may she rest in peace. A learned woman, whose house was always open to all. Rebbitzen Axelrod passed away on 15 Tammuz 5711, July 19, 1951. May her soul be bound up in the bond of everlasting life.

Historical Notes: Rabbi Axelrod was a charter member of the Beth Jacob Hebrew Parochial School for Girls of Baltimore which later became Bais Yaakov School for Girls.

Rebbitzen Yetta Taub

photo courtesy of Myrna Teck

Location: German Hill Cemetery, sometimes known as Hebrew Mt. Carmel, located near 6800 German Hill Road, Baltimore, MD. This cemetery has three portions. Two are located across from each other in the one–way portion of German Hill Road. This section is separated from the other two by Boston Street. The ohel is very near the caretaker's house on the section of German Hill Road that has traffic in both directions and is near Villager Circle.

Description: This is a gray cinder block building with a flat roof and no additional decoration. The six foot high doorway is covered by a much shorter metal gate. The burial plot inside is surrounded by cement. The interior rear wall has an inset memorial plaque. Candle boxes have been placed on the floor and on them are candles and books.

Dimensions: 7'– 4" x 12'– 9" x 6'– 4"

Condition: Overall condition appears good, but moisture seeps into the structure through the walls and roof.

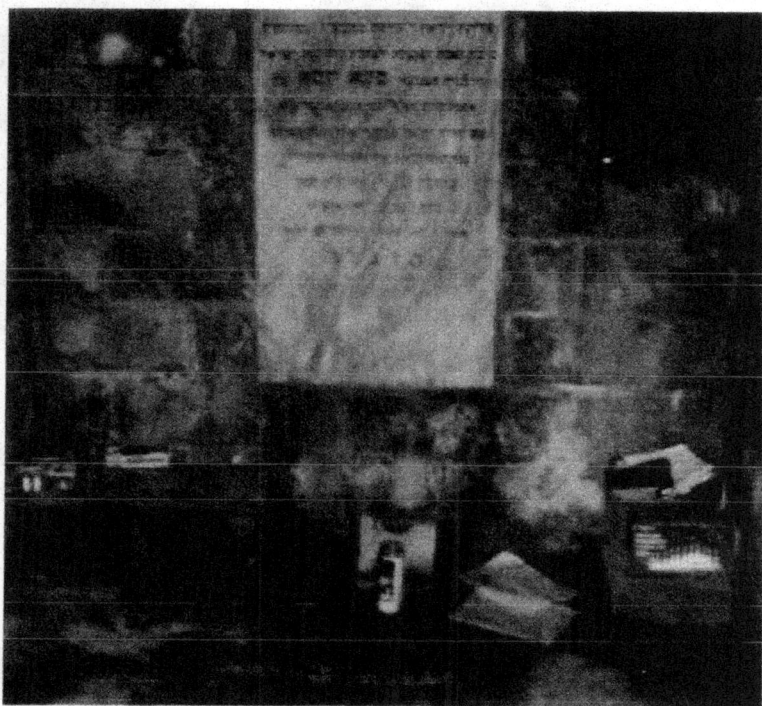

Notes from the plaque: A woman of valor, crown of her husband, parents and children, charitable and God–fearing, known for her good deeds, her discipline and intelligence; she worked for the purity and holiness of Israel. The modest Rebbitzen Fayga Yuta, may she rest in peace, wife of the righteous Rabbi Amrom Taub, may he live a long life. She was the daughter of the righteous Rabbi Yehiel Alter HaLevy and Basha. Rebbitzen Taub passed away to the great regret of her family and acquaintances in the prime of her life at the age of 38 on 7 Tevet 5724, December 23, 1963. Her deeds will not be forgotten and her memory will not end. May her soul be bound up in the bond of everlasting life.

Historical Notes: Several Baltimore ohelim include females who were interred with their spouses; however, this ohel was built solely to honor a woman.

The cemetery's caretaker, whose home is adjacent to the ohel, reports that Rebbitzen Taub's ohel is visited several times a year by groups of people.

Rebbitzen Yetta Taub was married to Rabbi Amrom Taub, who was sent to Baltimore to found a congregation in the 1950s by Satmar Rebbe, Rabbi Joel Teitelbaum.

A death notice in the *Baltimore Sun*, Dec. 24, 1963, refers to the Rebbitzen as Yetta (nee Steinberg) and below it is an expression of sympathy by The Ladies Auxiliary Bais Yaakov School for Girls, referring to her as Ita.

UNITED HEBREW CEMETERY

WASHINGTON BOULEVARD

Rabbi Reuben Rivkin

Location: United Hebrew Cemetery, Washington Boulevard and Sulphur Spring Road, Halethorpe, MD. This cemetery, located outside the Baltimore Beltway, is referred to as being in Baltimore rather than Halethorpe. The ohel is on the left side of the cemetery.

Description: This is a block building with roof of the same material. The rabbi's name is engraved above the door and above his name is engraved a Star of David. A bar on the door is bent, and the rear window pane is missing. The floor inside of the building is covered with green outdoor carpeting. No outline of the grave is visible. Cedar trees are on either side of the rear corners. A tree on the right corner is almost completely dead and a portion is leaning on the roof. The structure is believed to have been built by George Wilkinson and Co.

Dimensions: 6' x 7'–6" x 7'–2"

Condition: Good. According to the caretaker, the rear window has been vandalized twice.

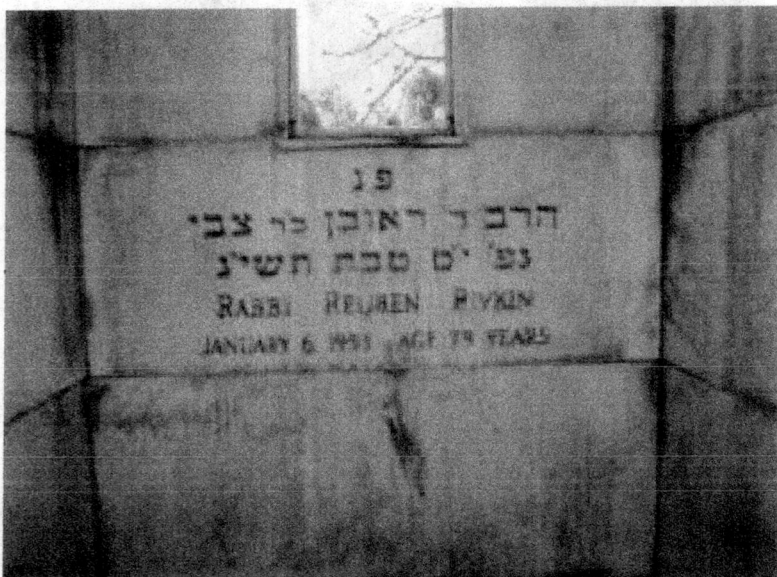

Notes from the inscription: Rabbi Reuven son of Zvi, passed away at age 79 on 19 Tevet 5713, January 6, 1953.

Historical Notes: According to *A Pictorial History of Maryland Jewry* by A. D. Glushakow, Rabbi Rivkin was among the leaders in the first decade of the Baltimore Mizrachi. The February 22, 1953, *Sun* obituary for Rabbi Rivkin noted he was a scholar and orator who came to the United States in 1906 from Kovno, Lithuania. He moved to Baltimore in 1914, where he served two congregations in south Baltimore before transferring to Aitz Chaim congregation.

The Maryland Historical Society has a negative of this structure in its Hughes photograph collection.

The September 15, 1954, *Baltimore News Post* had an article announcing the building's dedication.

Rabbi Nathan Kohen

Location: United Hebrew Cemetery, Washington Boulevard and Sulphur Spring Road, Halethorpe, MD. The cemetery, located just outside the Baltimore Beltway, is often referred to as being in Baltimore rather than Halethorpe. This ohel is close to the right hand boundary of the cemetery.

Description: The block and stucco building has a red roof with a hole in the right rear corner and other holes in the ceiling. Metal bars are on the side windows and doorway. A faint Star of David drawn in the stucco can be seen above the doorway. A crack runs from the left window to the roof. There is a memorial plaque with priestly hands on the inside back wall. There is a smooth area beneath the plaque which may indicate the place of a former sign or repair. Inside there is a cement floor and candles left by visitors.

Dimensions: 7' x 12' x 7'–5", doorway is 3'–6"

Condition: Poor

left side

Notes from the plaque: Here is buried the learned rabbi who spread Torah faithfully, our honored master and teacher, Rabbi Noach son of the distinguished Rabbi Yeshayahu Yehuda HaCohen. May he rest in peace. He served with distinction in the holy community of Rahitzin, Poland, for 14 years and some ten years at Anshe Emunah Synagogue in Baltimore. He left us suddenly at age 48 on the second day of Chol Hamoed Sukkot of 5699 [corresponds to 18 Tishrei], October 13, 1938. May his soul be bound up in the bond of everlasting life.

Historical Notes: The October 14, 1938, *Sun* reported that "Rabbi Kohen, who was born in Russia and educated at rabbinical colleges in Volozin and Kamenetz, came to Baltimore about 10 years ago. Rabbi Kohen died unexpectedly at his home on 522 South Hanover Street."

The grave of "Rebbitzen Esther Kahn, wife of Rabbi Noach Kohen," is located beside the ohel. Rebbitzen Esther passed away on December 19, 1979.

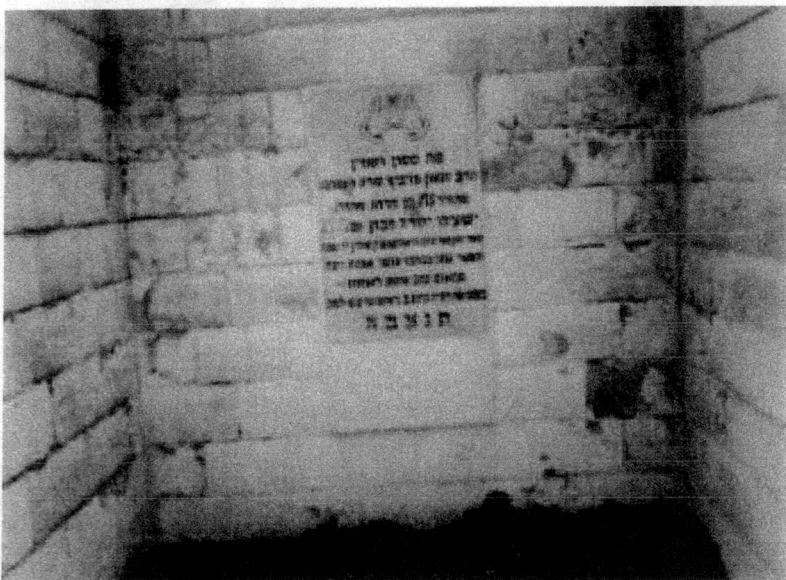

Rabbi Reuben S. Rabinowitz

Location: United Hebrew Cemetery, Washington Boulevard and Sulphur Spring Road, Halethorpe MD. Although the cemetery is located outside of the beltway in Halethorpe, it is often referred to as being in Baltimore. The building is near the center of the cemetery.

Description: The building is made of brick and stucco. A large chunk of stucco has fallen off the front and is lying on the ground. The ceiling has fallen down. There are barred windows on either side. A stone outline of the grave is visible with the rabbi's name engraved on the headstone. The door is missing and a tree is growing inside the building. In the spring leaves from the tree and vines cover the front entrance and wall.

At one time three plaques could be seen on Rabbi Rabinowitz's ohel, two of metal and one carved in marble. The metal plaques were connected to the front of the structure, with one on each side of the front door. The smaller of the two stated the name of the Chevra Kadisha that donated the ohel. The second metal plaque featured a memorial poem to the rabbi. The metal plaques are now missing, but earlier pictures of them appear below.

The inset marble tablet is still part of the outside, back wall. At the top a carving of scholars' books is clearly visible; however, the lettering is largely worn away and is nearly illegible.

It appears that the wording on the larger metal plaque was an English translation of what had been etched into the marble.

Dimensions: 8' x 11'x 7'–8"

photo courtesy of Myrna Teck, date unknown

Condition: interior condition is poor and part of front stucco has pulled away.

Notes from the plaques: The photo on the previous page shows the smaller metal plaque which had fallen to the ground. At one time it had been affixed to the front of the structure. It read in Hebrew: "This ohel was donated by the Chevra Kadisha of Aitz Chaim Congregation in the year 5698 [1938]."

The photo on the next page is of the second metal plaque. The picture of it was taken as it rested on the floor of the ohel. The plaque, which was in English, is no longer there, but the text was as follows:

Rabbi Rabinowitz
This mausoleum donated by
Chevra Kadisha of Cong. Etz Chaim
In the year 1938

A saint on whom rests the moral foundations of the universe.
By whose wisdom the secrets of the world are revealed.
His is the source of the living waters of Torah.
Who increases the heritage of ethical life for the myriad
Of willing devotees.
With whose image now gone depletes the sacred quality of our community.
His righteousness goes before him, for God's honor has he
Earned on earth.
Our loving father the leader of our flock our spiritual mentor.
The chain of traditional aristocracy the revered example
For an admiring generation.
Rabbi Reuben Zelig Rabinowitz, son of the scion Isaiah.
In the year born 5608 (1847) and died with a good name in the year 5652 (1891).
May his soul be bound up in the bonds of eternity.
This memorial is dedicated in memory of daughter, Sarah by grandchildren Rubin, Selig, Hattie, Minnie.

photo courtesy of Myrna Teck (date unknown)

Although the above now–missing plaque stated that Rabbi Rabinowitz died in 1891, it is believed that 1892 is the correct year based on the January 6, 1892, obituary in the *Sun* paper. [Death date corresponds to 5 Tevet 5652.]

A picture of the back wall of the ohel appears on the following page. The worn–down Hebrew lettering which was carved into the marble is under the carving of books.

Historical Notes: According to the January 6, 1892, *Sun* newspaper, "Rabbi Reuben S. Rabinowitz of the Polish Synagogue died yesterday morning at his home. Rabbi Rabinowitz was born in Russ–Poland forty–three years ago. He came to the United States twelve years ago and for eight years he resided in New York. For the last four years he had been rabbi of the synagogues on North High and North Exeter Streets."

The January 11, 1892, *Sun* newspaper reported that memorial services were held for Rabbi Rabinowitz at the High Street Synagogue where "Rev. Dr. Lowenthal of Philadelphia delivered an eloquent panegyric on the life and work of the deceased rabbi."

Outside back wall

79

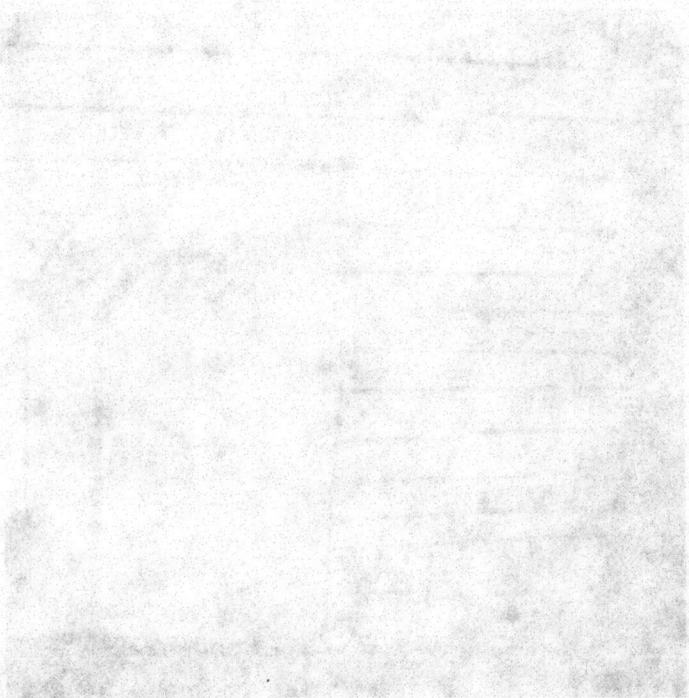

Visiting the Ohelim

The ohelim photographed in this booklet can be found in five of the old Jewish cemeteries in Baltimore. Most of these cemeteries are located close to one another, thus a visit to all the ohelim could easily be accomplished in a morning or afternoon. Eight of the ohelim can be found in Rosedale, a large cemetery used by many congregations and organizations.

Less than two miles from Rosedale, two other ohelim can be found in the cemetery at Bowley's Lane. Less than three miles from Bowley's Lane is the B'nai Israel Cemetery on Southern Avenue with four more ohelim. Thus, fourteen ohelim are within five miles of each other. The remaining five ohelim are in two cemeteries. Two are in the cemeteries located on German Hill Road, and three can be found in The United Hebrew Cemetery on Washington Boulevard. The list below demonstrates the mileage between the cemeteries.

Rosedale to Bowley's Lane:	1.92 miles
Bowley's Lane to Southern Avenue:	2.91 miles
Southern Avenue to German Hill Road	5.72 miles
Rosedale to German Hill Road:	4.28 miles
Rosedale to Washington Boulevard:	13.65 miles

List of Ohelim By Date of Death

Key: B=B'nai Israel; G=German Hill Road; H=Herring Run–Bowley's
Lane; R=Rosedale Cemetery; W=Washington Boulevard

In some cases, English dates will be one day earlier than the
Hebrew date if the person died after sundown.

Death Date: English (Hebrew)	Name and Cemetery
Jan. 5, 1892 (5 Tevet 5652)	Rabbi Reuben S. Rabinowitz (W)
Jun. 8, 1912 (23 Sivan 5672)	Rabbi Abraham Levinson (B)
Jun. 25, 1914 (1 Tammuz 5674)	Joseph Fisher (B)
Aug. 31, 1918 (23 Elul 5678)	Jacob Benesch (R)
Nov. 8, 1919 (15 Cheshvan 5680)	Rabbi Solomon Kruger (H)
Dec. 31, 1919 (9 Tevet 5680)	Isreal Rivkin (R)
Apr. 14, 1928 (24 Nissan 5688)	Fannie Rivkin (R)
Sept. 28, 1928 (14 Tishrei 5689)	Samuel Fisher ((B)
Oct. 4, 1929 (1 Tishrei 5690)	Annie Fisher (B)
Jan. 5, 1930 (5 Tevet 5690)	Rabbi Morris Marcus (R)
Aug. 4, 1931 (21 Av 5691)	Rabbi I.B. Isaacson (R)
Mar. 25, 1932 (17 Adar II 5692)	Rebbitzen Chava Isaacson (R)
Jun. 12, 1932 (8 Sivan 5692)	Rabbi Israel Zvi Karen (R)
Jul. 28, 1932 (24 Tammuz 5692)	Rabbi Joseph Jacob Marcus (B)
Jan. 25, 1934 (9 Shevat 5694)	Yehuda Moshe Barrash (R)
Dec. 19, 1936 (5 Tevet 5697)	Rebbitzen Gittel Kruger (H)

Death Date: English (Hebrew)	Name and Cemetery
Feb. 4, 1937 (23 Shevat 5697)	Rabbi Abraham Schwartz (R)
Dec. 9, 1937 (5 Tevet 5698)	Ida Lipsitz (B)
Oct. 13, 1938 (18 Tishrei 5699)	Rabbi Nathan Kohen (W)
Mar. 5, 1940 (25 Adar I 5700)	Rabbi Moshe Rabinowitz (H)
Dec. 25, 1940 (25 Kislev 5701)	Rabbi Samuel Liebb (R)
Jan. 24, 1942 (6 Shevat 5702)	Israel Benesch (R)
Nov. 7, 1944 (21 Cheshvan 5705)	Harry Lipsitz (B)
Aug. 30, 1950 (17 Elul 5710)	Sarah Barrash (R)
Jul. 19, 1951 (15 Tammuz 5711)	Rebbitzen Bracha Axelrod (G)
Mar. 1, 1952 (4 Adar 5712)	Rabbi A.E. Axelrod (G)
Jan. 6, 1953 (19 Tevet 5713)	Rabbi Reuben Rivkin (W)
May 13, 1955 (21 Iyar 5715)	Rebbitzen Ida Mihaly (R)
May 16, 1955 (24 Iyar 5715)	Alta Sarah Rivkah Marcus (B)
Apr. 19, 1957 (18 Nissan 5717)	Rabbi Hillel Mihaly (R)
May 3, 1957 (2 Iyar 5717)	Rebbitzen Esther Rabinowitz (H)
Dec. 23, 1963 (7 Tevet 5724)	Rebbitzen Yetta Taub (G)

Bibliography

1. Collins–Kreiner, Noga. "Graves as attractions: pilgrimage–tourism to Jewish holy graves in Israel." *Journal of Cultural Geography 24.1 (2006): 67+*. Gale databases accessed 19 Mar. 2010 via Anne Arundel County Public Library.

2. Gellis, Rabbi Israel, *Carta's Guide to Tombs of the Righteous in the Land of Israel*. Carta, Jerusalem, 2008. (Hebrew)

3. Goldin, Hyman E., *Hamadrikh: The Rabbi's Guide, A Manual of Jewish Religious Rituals, Ceremonials and Customs*. NY: Hebrew Publishing Company, 1939.

4. Glushakow, A.D., ed., *A Pictorial History of Maryland Jewry*. Baltimore, MD: Jewish Voice Publishing Co., 1955.

5. Lamm, Maurice, *The Jewish Way in Death and Mourning*. NY: Jonathan David Publishers, 1969.

6. Menachemson, Nolan, *A Practical Guide to Jewish Cemeteries*. Bergenfield, NJ: Avotaynu, 2007.

7. Pruce, Earl, *Synagogues, Temples, and Congregations of Maryland, 1830–1990*. Baltimore, MD: The Jewish Historical Society of Maryland, Inc., 1993.

8. Rabinowicz, Rabbi Tzvi, *A Guide to Life: Jewish Laws and Customs of Mourning*. Northvale, NJ: Jason Aronson Inc., 1989.

9. Segal, Joshua L., Rabbi, *For an Eternal Memory: Ordinary and Unusual Jewish Cemetery Monuments and How*

to Create Them. Nashua, NH: Jewish Cemetery Publishing, 2009.

10. Segal, Joshua L., Rabbi, *A Field Guide to Visiting a Jewish Cemetery.* Nashua, NH: Jewish Cemetery Publishing, 2005.

11. Silberman, Lauren, *Images of America: The Jewish Community of Baltimore.* Charleston, SC: Arcadia Publishing, 2008.

www.ingramcontent.com/pod-product-compliance
Lightning Source LLC
Chambersburg PA
CBHW070857280326
41934CB00008B/1472

* 9 780788 452918 *